# 8 Keys to Becoming A Great Leader

## With Leadership Lessons and Tips From Gibbs, Yoda and Capt'n Jack Sparrow

By

Steven B. Howard

# 8 Keys to Becoming A Great Leader

**©2016 Steven B. Howard**
All rights reserved.
ISBN: 978-1-943702-24-4 (Print edition)
   978-1-943702-25-1 (Kindle edition)

No part of this Book may be reproduced or transmitted in any form or by any means, electronic or mechanical, including photocopying, recording, faxing, emailing, posting online, or by any information storage and retrieval system, without prior written permission from the Author.

For reprint permission, please contact:
   Steven B. Howard
   c/o Caliente Press
   1775 E Palm Canyon Drive, Suite 110-198
   Palm Springs, CA  92264
   U.S.A
   Email: steven@CalienteLeadership.com

Published by:
   Caliente Press
   1775 E Palm Canyon Drive, Suite 110-198
   Palm Springs, CA 92264
   U.S.A.
   Email: CalientePress@verizon.net

Cover Design:  Zachery Colman

# Dedication

*This book is dedicated to*

*Patricia A. Ward*

*A life-long friend, confidante, and supporter.*

*Many thanks.*

# Table of Contents

| | |
|---|---|
| Introduction | 7 |
| 1. Meet Our Leadership Brain Trust | 11 |
| 2. Great Leadership Requires Beliefs, Mindset and Behaviors | 19 |
| 3. Leading Teams and People | 39 |
| 4. Leading People Development | 51 |
| 5. Leading For Results | 61 |
| 6. Ensuring Accountability | 75 |
| 7. Communicating As A Leader | 91 |
| 8. Great Leadership Is An Art | 99 |
| Appendix | |
|     My Personal Leadership Philosophy | 111 |
|     The Rules of Great Leadership | 113 |
|     Gibbs Rules | 117 |
|     Yoda Quotes | 121 |
|     Capt'n Jack Sparrow Quotes | 129 |
| About the Author | 133 |

# Introduction

The old school of leadership is just that — old school. Gone are the days of Control and Command leaders in the workplace. And, to a lesser degree, gone too are the days of dominant personality leadership.

Sure, there are exceptions to these changes. But for the most part critical leadership skills have segued into a focus on behaviors and actions over traits, titles and "looking the part." As today's pity saying goes, "you don't have to have a title to be a leader."

This focus on the behaviors and actions of leaders is often paired with an understanding that leaders are made, not born, and that anyone, at any level within an organization, can be (and is) a leader.

One of the key challenges facing leaders is knowing when to be a leader, and when to be a manager. Management and leadership each comprise a set of distinct behavioral skills and responsibilities. These are not style changes or personality traits that can be flipped on and off like a light switch.

As Linda E. Ginzel, clinical professor of managerial psychology at the University of Chicago Booth School of Management wrote, "Recognize that what matters is not whether you fit into some leadership suit of clothes or match up to some template of a leader personality. What matters is how you choose to behave."

Adds Roger Trapp, in an article in *Forbes*, "This distinction is crucial because, unlike traits, behaviors form the basis for skills, and skills can be practiced." Additionally, skills can be developed and learned.

The other foundation for great leaders is having an understanding their own leadership platform — a set of beliefs, values and personal rules related to the kind of leader they want to be. This foundation drives the workplace environment and climate of the team any leader leads.

I believe that great leadership is an art.

It is the art of achieving progress through the involvement and actions of others. This is why great leaders are strong in both leading people and leading for results, while good leaders typically lead only one or the other.

In *8 Keys to Becoming A Great Leader* I use three icons from pop culture — Special Agent Leroy Jethro Gibbs from the hit television series *NCIS*, Jedi Master Yoda from the *Star Wars* movie series, and swashbuckling Captain Jack Sparrow from the *Pirates of the Caribbean* series of movies — to demonstrate my 8 Keys to Great Leadership model:

- Personal Leadership Philosophy
- Leadership Mindset
- Core Set of Leadership Behaviors Aligned With Organization's Culture
- Leading Teams and People
- Leading People Development
- Leading For Results
- Ensuring Accountability
- Communicating as a Leader

The results from this leadership development approach are performance enhancement, better leveraging and utilization of existing leadership skills, enhanced communications as a leader, increased team member engagement, and greater consistency in leadership behaviors congruent with the organization's brand and culture.

Combining consistent behavioral actions with a personal leadership philosophy creates *great leadership*. These are the leaders who not only get results, but do so while building and enhancing the climate of their respective organizations, continuously developing the skills of themselves and their team members, and simultaneously creating new leaders (not just followers).

While there are many books exuding how particular individuals have risen to the task of leadership in the business, military and political worlds, there are few that have examined how some of our pop culture icons have exhibited the characteristics of great leadership.

In a discussion with my two adult sons on the merits of the teachings of the *Star* Wars character Yoda, they countered that the sayings of Jack Sparrow in the *Pirates of the Caribbean* series had more meaning to them. Reflecting upon this discussion a few days later I decided this was an interesting topic bearing further investigation. At first I thought this might just be a generational cultural divide that could be surmounted.

However, when I widened my scope of thinking to include The Rules of Gibbs from the long-running hit TV show *NCIS*, the concept of how leadership is portrayed on screen by fictional characters became a new focus. Not having the time to explore leadership behaviors and philosophies across the entire spectrum of pop culture, I elected to simply focus on these three as illustrative examples.

My purpose here is not to suggest that any or all of these fictional characters make ideal leaders, but rather to use their behaviors and leadership platforms as a launching pad for readers to look into and develop their own leadership beliefs, skills and behaviors.

Hopefully you will find some nuggets of useful wisdom within these pages that are relevant to your current or future leadership challenges and desires.

And, if nothing else, please have a bit of fun as you see what tips and lessons Leroy Jethro Gibbs, Yoda and Capt'n Jack Sparrow have for you on leadership.

Best wishes for continued success.


Steven B. Howard
July 2016

# Meet Our Leadership Brain Trust

## Special Agent Gibbs

Leroy Jethro Gibbs is the leader of the investigative team of the long-running, highly rated *NCIS* show on CBS and syndicated worldwide.

Reporting to the Director of NCIS (Naval Criminal Investigative Services), Gibbs leads a team of three federal agents, two pathologists and a forensics lab scientist.

Portrayed by the ruggedly handsome former collegiate quarterback Mark Harmon, the character Gibbs has the stoic nature of a U.S. Marine Corps Scout Sniper combined with intuitive leadership skills. These qualities help ensure a successful resolution of each case that comes his team's way. His rugged, hard-nosed command and control leadership style drives results, while his boyish charm and deep-seated commitment to his team members builds team loyalty.

Probably due to his military background and loyalty to the Marine Corps, Gibbs tends to react aggressively and hostilely whenever he confronts someone in a position of power, trust or authority who has misused that position for personal gain. His is rigidly firm in this area, even when the person is a former friend or colleague.

Unlike many of the main protagonists in TV shows, Gibbs is far from perfect. His flaws include an addiction for coffee and a history of poor choices in women (he has been widowed once and divorced three times). He also exhibits an extraordinary level of personal resentment toward his father, particularly in early seasons of the show. They do, however, reach a level of reconciliation and mutual respect before his father passes away.

A natural-born leader, his leadership talents were hardened by the discipline, rigidity and structure of his Marine Corps career. These make him a strong leader, but not necessarily an ideal leadership role model for today's world.

On the other hand, Gibbs is an HR officer's nightmare, with his sarcastic comments to team members, head-slapping of subordinates and the tendency to bend (and sometimes step over) the rules and regulations governing federal officers.

Speaking of rules, Gibbs has his own set of numbered rules, which are quoted frequently in the weekly episodes (see Appendix for the full set of the Gibbs Rules known to date).

If nothing else, Gibbs is who he is and his leadership actions and behaviors are totally congruent with his personal leadership philosophy and those famed Gibbs Rules.

### Jedi Master Yoda

The legendary Jedi Master Yoda lived for nearly 900 years, first appearing in the 1980 film *The Empire Strikes Back*. A member of the Jedi High Council, he is one of the oldest and most famous Jedi Masters in the *Star Wars* universe.

In the original *Star Wars* trilogy Yoda trains Luke Skywalker to fight against the Galactic Empire. From the very first film Yoda immediately gain pop culture cult status for his unique speaking style and his memorable sayings.

In the prequel films Yoda appears as the Grand Master of the Jedi Order, as well as a high-ranking general of clone troopers. Interestingly, the face of Yoda was partly based on that of Albert Einstein.

Though small in stature (approximately 26 inches tall and weighing just under 29 pounds according to the online *Star Wars* Wikipedia), Yoda was renowned within the Jedi Order for his insightful wisdom, powers of the Force and his lightsaber combat abilities.

*Star Wars* series creator George Lucas purposely kept many details of Yoda's background and history unknown, including the character's race and home world. All we know is that Yoda belonged to an ancient and mysterious species.

The character's unique speaking style and wise words of wisdom make him both popular and memorable with *Star Wars* fans. His speech syntax was described as object-subject-word order, though this sentence structure was not used consistently in all his screen appearances.

In 2007 Yoda was named the 28th greatest movie character of all time by *Empire*, the UK's most popular film magazine. He was also selected 60th on a list of the 100 Greatest Fictional Characters at the website Fandonmania.com.

Today, a life-size statue of Yoda greets visitors at the Lucasfilm's Letterman Digital Arts Center in San Francisco's Presidio, the headquarters of famed motion picture visual effects studio Industrial Light and Magic.

**Captain Jack Sparrow**
The main protagonist in Disney's *Pirates of the Caribbean* film series, Captain Jack Sparrow is one of the nine pirate leaders of the Brethren Court.

An ingenious, witty and fun-loving character, Sparrow is played by Johnny Depp. Apparently Depp based his portrayal of Sparrow on Rolling Stones guitarist Keith Richards and the cartoon character Pepé Le Pew (a striped skunk that strolls the streets of Paris looking for love). Richards, by the way, appears twice in cameo roles as Sparrow's father Edward Teague.

As one of the Pirate Leaders of the Seven Seas, Captain Sparrow is well known by both the pirate community and the British Navy trying to maintain lawful order throughout the

Caribbean Sea. He is also well liked — and highly disliked — by powerful members of both communities.

Prone to being taken captive by both sides, Sparrow consistently escapes his entanglements through wit and negotiations. He also has an uncanny ability to enlist the help of both loyal crew members and adversaries turned into collaborators.

A man of wit and trickery, Sparrow excels at turning his foes against one another. Unlike most pirates, he also prefers negotiations over combat, using his intelligence and analytical skills to prevent physical disputes. When such conflict avoidance techniques fail to work, Sparrow is an excellent conflict management leader who gets opposing sides to put down their swords and see the big picture, and how collaboration might attain this higher objective.

In many ways Captain Sparrow is an ethical pirate, with a unique mixture of honorableness and unlawfulness. It is hard to call this renegade pirate evil, even though he often oversteps the boundaries of the law (both British law and pirate law). He is more the swashbuckling, happy-go-lucky, live-for-today iconoclastic hero Hollywood audiences adore.

He is neither totally honorable nor pure evil. For Sparrow, veracity is a tool to be used only when warranted or when necessary to move others toward a desired outcome.

Falsehoods, lies, deceit, and half-truths are likewise equally used as similar tools.

Sparrow struggles to understand his own moral code and what it takes to be a moral person. He undoubtedly sees little difference between the rich, colonizing barons of the East India Trading Company and his pirate brethren. Both are plunders of riches and enslavers of men; though one has the law on its side and the other does not.

Sparrow is also a master of self-promotion and self-interest. His personal brand is one of marvelous escapes, wanton treachery and legendary exploits. All of which he is happy to regale any willing listeners with his fabulous tales and stories.

Captain Jack Sparrow was named the eighth greatest movie character of all time by movie magazine *Empire*. And a 2015 poll by *Empire* placed Sparrow as the 14th greatest film character.

While Sparrow's moral and ethical code are not leadership traits we espouse to our readers or clients, his actions and behaviors, along with some of his words of wisdom, do provide leaders a valid reference guide in agility, adaptability and using course corrections to attain desired goals.

Interestingly, Sparrows First Mate and most trusted comrade is Joshamee Gibbs. A coincidence? Perhaps. Who knows? On the other hand, Rule 39 from Special Agent Gibbs states, "There is no such thing as coincidence."

# Great Leadership Requires Beliefs, Mindset and Behaviors

Great leadership is an art.

It is the art of achieving progress through the involvement and actions of others.

Great leaders perform this art, and attain desired results, by having a personal leadership philosophy, the right leadership mindset, and through using the right tools and techniques. They are also consistent in their leadership behaviors.

A leadership philosophy is a set of core beliefs and principles about leadership and the type of leader you want to be.

A leadership mindset, while closely related, is different. A leadership mindset is a set of core values upon which leadership behaviors are based.

Combining these two sets of beliefs creates a foundation that will drive the organizational environment and climate of the team a leader leads, whether this is a four-person department or a multinational company with hundreds of thousands of employees.

There are many ways to create your own personal leadership philosophy and leadership mindset. You could have your own set of rules (like Gibbs), your own overriding philosophy of what is right (Yoda), or know how you will act under pressure and changing circumstances (Sparrow).

Let's look at each of these in more detail.

**Leadership Philosophy**
A leadership philosophy is a set of beliefs and principles that strongly influences how you interpret reality and guides how you react to people, events and situations. Research has shown that consistent leadership behavior and actions require a clear personal leadership philosophy.

A written leadership philosophy helps leaders demonstrate and communicate to team members and others what they expect, what they value and how they will act in any given situation. This helps to make their workplace environment less stressful and more productive, as well as keeping them on track and aligned with their core beliefs and values.

Having a written personal leadership philosophy is one of the distinctions between great leaders and average leaders.

Konosuke Matsushita, the founder of Panasonic in Japan, is known in that country as the "god of management" for his writings and speeches on leadership and management. He wrote, "If you are a leader, you must have an ideology of leadership. If you lack an ideology, and attempt to decide everything on a case-by-case basis, you will never be capable of strong leadership."

When a leader is consistent, they are able to inspire trust; whereas an inconsistent leader causes confusion, anxiety, angst, and uncertainty within their troops.

As you can tell, it is extremely important that leaders gain clarity about their own leadership philosophy, style and behavior.

## Developing Your Personal Leadership Philosophy

Great leaders know and understand their beliefs, values and personal rules of leadership. Your personal leadership philosophy drives the workplace environment and climates of the teams you lead.

No single leadership philosophy can be viable for everyone. Each leader is faced with different circumstances, brings different backgrounds to their leadership position and leads widely different teams of people. Hence you have to figure out what the right leadership philosophy and mindset is for you.

Stop and ask yourself, "What is your personal leadership philosophy?" When was the last time you paused and seriously gave this question sufficient reflection? If it has been awhile, read our article on why it is important to have a written leadership philosophy. You will find the article, and others, under the Resources Tab on our company website at www.CalienteLeadership.com.

There are seven sets of questions to ask yourself in developing, reviewing or fine-tuning your personal leadership philosophy:

1. What is the primary focus of your leadership beliefs — results, people, both? Why?

2. What do you want to accomplish in your current leadership role and as your career advances? Why?

3. How would you like others to describe your leadership style and behaviors? With what specific words and terms?

4. What do you expect from those you lead? How will you demonstrate and communicate this?

5. What level of control makes you comfortable? What level of delegation makes you comfortable? Why?

6. How do you view the mistakes of others? Of yourself? Why?

7. What are your personal rules of leadership? Are these written down? Are these rigid or flexible?

For your reference, I have shared my personal rules of great leadership in the appendix at the end of this book. These are instrumental components of my personal leadership philosophy.

**Leadership Mindset**

Some of the core values you may want to include in your personal leadership mindset philosophy could be: confidence, adaptability, focus on people development, having a realistic vision. The important thing is that the values must be your own — things you deeply believe in and care about. They cannot just be a list of positive attributes that you find in a book or online.

No matter what attributes and values you choose, however, trust overrides them all. Without trust, none of your other attributes and values matter. Trust is something you earn and maintain through your behaviors. It is not bestowed upon you by rank or title.

Confidence is another key element of a strong leadership mindset. It comes from knowing yourself, and fully understanding (and appreciating) your strengths and weaknesses.

It also comes from observing and analyzing how you make decisions, both good and bad. Not every decision will work out as you expect. That's okay. The key is to reflect back on how and why you made a particular decision to learn about your decision-making capabilities and tendencies. This helps you grow as a leader and gives you greater confidence when you have to make judgment calls in areas where you may not be a technical subject matter expert.

This also enables you to de-personalize decisions, i.e. no more "I'll go with Beth on this one." Decisions should be made based on your determination of the facts and reality of the situation, not based on which person is presenting a proposed option.

It also allows you to create your own solutions from differing opinions that build on the strengths and ideas of each. Leveraging positive cognitive conflict (i.e. the opposing of two or more ideas) is one of the best ways of coming up with innovative solutions. It also keeps negative personal conflict from getting in the way of good decision making.

## Leadership Behaviors

Where do most of us learn our parenting skills? Usually from our own parents, and the parents of our spouse.

The same holds true for learning leadership skills. For most of us, this comes from observing the leaders and managers we have worked for or observed in action. We tend to cherry-pick the skills of those leaders that we personally liked, and pledge not to repeat the behaviors that we considered to be mistakes, irritations or distasteful.

There are two problems with this approach.

First, if the behaviors of the leaders we have worked with and observed over time have been more hands-on managerial in nature, then we will likely exhibit similar tendencies. Secondly, we are making decisions based on behaviors that we personally like or prefer, without taking into account if these behaviors are best suited for the team members that we lead.

You can overcome this by contemplating your own leadership philosophy and the skill sets and leadership behaviors required to remain in alignment with your beliefs and values.

By creating your own leadership mindset philosophy, and then identifying the behaviors that will help you implement these guiding principles, you will avoid the trap of deciding everything on a case-by-case basis. This results in consistency of leadership behavior; a benefit for both you and your team members.

To illustrate, let's look as some of the core principles and values that our three fictional characters seem to have:

**Gibbs**

> Trust your instincts.
>
> Official rules are guidelines — push boundaries but don't break.
>
> Have personal rules in writing.
>
> Success comes from teamwork.

**Yoda**

> Leadership means teaching others.
>
> Must be focused — future focused.
>
> Continuous improvement is key.
>
> Be cautious of the Dark Side of leadership.

**Sparrow**

> You must have the courage to act.
>
> Pragmatism above all.
>
> Keep the Big Goal in mind at all times. (Lose a battle, but not the war.)
>
> Leadership, like life, is a journey.
>
> It's all about having the right attitude.
>
> It's okay to have some fun in the process.

The core values of Special Agent Gibbs are, of course, encapsulated in his set of rules. Four of these rules give us insight into his leadership mindset:

> Don't believe what you're told. Double check. (Rule 3)
>
> Never be unreachable. (A second Rule 3)
>
> Bend the line, don't break it. (Rule 14)
>
> It's better to seek forgiveness than ask permission. (Rule 18)

Followers of the *NCIS* show can readily see how these four leadership mindset rules translate into the actions taken by Gibbs, and his team, in episode after episode.

There is another component of the Gibbs mindset that, though not written down as a stipulated rule, certainly explains his leadership behavior. This is revealed when he tells of one his agents, in the *Hung Out To Dry* episode, "Don't work the system when you can work the people."

As a former Marine, Gibbs believes strongly in the chain of command. In the episode *Switch* he tells Officer Ziva David, who recently joined his team on a temporary posting from the Israeli Mossad intelligence agency, "In my country, on my team, working my cases, my people don't bypass the chain of command."

On the other hand, as an action-oriented, results-driven leader, Gibbs does not always believe in, or agree with, the rules and procedures laid down by those in authority, especially if these get in the way of his team's success. Hence Rule 14 on bending lines but not breaking them.

While I would not advocate the leadership style of Gibbs for use with today's workforce and in real-life organizations, my point here is that his firmly entrenched, and self understood, leadership philosophy and leadership mindset are totally congruent with his leadership behavior. Such congruency is one of the important differentiators between good leaders and great leaders. And Gibbs is definitely a great leader, at least by my reckoning.

Yoda is also highly congruent in his leadership thinking and advice, which is mostly focused on personal leadership development and communication. His core values include self confidence and digging deeply into one's inner strengths.

Statements from Yoda that give us an insight into his leadership mindset include:

*Feel the Force!*

*You will only find what you bring in.*

His leadership mindset is also revealed when he responds to Luke Skywalker's comment "I cannot believe it," with a deeply felt "That is why you fail." Yoda's lesson here for leaders is that one must have faith and confidence in themselves, and their abilities, in order to be successful.

Such inner belief and confidence applies to all leaders. In great leaders we not only find deeper convictions and a stronger sense of self confidence, but we also see an ability to tap into these leadership mindset components when most needed.

Capt'n Jack Sparrow, in many ways, combines the need to act within the parameters of a personal code (ala Gibbs) with a leadership philosophy and leadership mindset based on thoughtful thinking and tangible experiences (ala Yoda).

Sparrow's leadership code of conduct, of course, is rooted in the formal Code of the Pirate Brethren. More commonly known as the Pirate's Code, this was the code of conduct among pirates of the 17$^{th}$ and 18$^{th}$ centuries. Although an important set of rules sworn to under oath, many pirates, Sparrow included, tended to treat the Pirate's Code more as a flexible set of guidelines.

The fictional character Sparrow in Disney's *Pirates of the Caribbean* movie series has a more worldly and humanitarian philosophy than what one suspects would have been found in most real swashbuckling pirates. We see this in how he treats his crew, his loyalty to key crew members and as well in what he says:

*Not all treasure is silver and gold mate.*

*Better to not know which moments may be your last, alive to the mystery of it all.*

*Remember, he who fights and runs away, lives to run away again.*

*It's not the destination so much as the journey, they say.*

This lovable pirate also exudes extreme confidence in his own abilities (almost as if he had been trained by Yoda!): "The seas may be rough, but I am the Captain! No matter how difficult, I will always prevail."

Of course, Captain Sparrow is still a pirate and true to his calling of the pirate life. As such not all his leadership statements represent the egalitarian concept of the greater good for the greater many. After all, his most famous quote is: "Take what you can. Give nothing back."

A complicated man and leader, the most important element of Sparrow's leadership philosophy seems to be, "The only rules that really matter are these: what a man can do and what a man can't do." In many ways that also sums up the tips and lessons from both Gibbs and Yoda.

Who knew that a NCIS Special Agent, a Jedi Master and a buccaneer pirate had so much in common? And who knew that these three fictional characters had so much to show us about leadership? Well, now we do.

## Managers vs. Leaders

A leadership role is significantly different from a manager role.

These differences may have been best summarized by leading management thinker Peter Drucker, "Managers do things right. Leaders do the right things."

Another distinction is that managers will say "go do this" to their subordinates, whereas leaders will be heard saying "let's go do this."

Specific differences between managers and leaders include:

| **Managers** | **Leaders** |
|---|---|
| Accept the status quo. | Challenge the status quo. |
| Ensure all practices, policies and procedures get put into operations. | Create and articulate visions and strategies. |
| Focus on the tactical and the short term. | Focus on the strategic and the long term |
| Tell subordinates what to do and how to do it, without seeking input from those handling the implementation. | Set direction, obtain buy-in from others, and allow the "how to" to be developed by those handing implementation. |
| Managing work. | |

| | |
|---|---|
| Plan, organize and coordinate. | Leading people. |
| Deal with change on a reactive basis. | Lead, inspire, motivate, and engage. |
| | Initiate change proactively. |

For those in first-line or first time supervisory and leadership positions, one of the hardest tasks is jugging these managerial and leadership activities. Most leaders are required to alternate hats between moments when they need to use managerial behaviors and when they need to perform as a leader.

This balancing act is further complicated if they also have their own individual contributor responsibilities to deliver.

Gordon Tredgold, in a May 31, 2016 article in *Inc.* identified what he calls the 7 Deadly Sins of First-Time Leaders:

- Creating too much distance between the leader and his or her team.
- Becoming too friendly or familiar with team members, which may impact the need to make tough decisions down the road.
- Thinking they need to provide all the answers.
- Being too hands on, particularly in identifying implementation steps.
- Taking too much personal credit for the work being done.
- Overly relying on control instead of influence.

- Displaying a lack of confidence in the team or individuals by micro managing.

New leaders also tend to cling and hold onto projects and responsibilities longer than necessary, often thinking that doing so shows they are a hard worker and worthy of future promotion. A good leader cannot afford to hold onto projects and programs after they have achieved initial objectives. As Gibbs Rule #11 states, "When the job is done, walk away."

Great leaders are constantly focused on future opportunities and challenges, instead of relishing past accomplishments and reminding others of what they have achieved in the past.

While managers are rightfully focused on tasks, processes, procedures, and policies, leaders need to additionally concentrate on the people aspect of the business. As U.S. Navy Rear Admiral Grace Murray Hopper stated, "You manage things. You lead people."

We would add that leaders, especially great leaders, also lead people development, a topic we will cover in more detail in chapter four.

Going from being a manager to becoming a leader is all about mindset...where you place your focus and attention...and whether your mental focus is about getting things done or about leading people to achieve results.

This requires an emphasis of five critical leadership behaviors that impact sustainable success for any organization:

- Leading People and Teams
- Leading for Results
- Ensuring Accountability
- Communicating as a Leader
- Leading Continuous People Development

These five leadership focus areas will help you to create a high-performing climate for the portion of the organization you lead.

Many research studies have proven that leaders who create a positive workplace climate achieve more stellar results than leaders who do not. One of the most cited of such studies, by the Hay Group, showed that:

- A positive climate will increase results by up to 30%.
- A poor climate is virtually a guarantee of poor performance.
- 50% to 70% of variance in organizational climate can be explained by differences in leadership styles.

It is also well documented that the maxim "people leave bosses, not organizations" is excruciatingly true. Unfortunately this results in tremendous costs to organizations to replace good employees who leave due to the unsatisfying climate they find in their departments and work teams.

## Results Focus or People Focus?

You may now be asking yourself, are great leaders more focused on results or people? Which makes the better leader, a no-nonsense, drive-home-the-results type or the motivational, let's-put-people-first style?

Well, in 2009 James Zenger published an extraordinary study of 60,000 employees in an attempt to answer this question. His survey was designed to identify if different characteristics of a leader affected whether employees perceived the leader as a great leader or not.

The results of his study were astonishing and crystal clear. If a leader was perceived by his or her staff as being strongly results focused, then that leader was seen as a great leader only 14% of the time. Likewise, if a leader was perceived by his or staff as being strongly focused on people, then that leader was seen as a great leader only 12% of the time.

However, those leaders who displayed a balanced approach and focus on both results and people, were perceived as great leaders a phenomenal 72% of the time. So the answer to the question of results focus vs. people focus is not either one or the other, but clearly a combination of both.

This has certainly been true of the great leaders I have worked under, consulted, or coached.

**Pulling It All Together**
Great leaders know full well that performance results and change implementation are actually best derived by the engagement and motivation of team members, particularly those who receive continuous skill development.

The best leaders are people who lead from their own personal strengths, leadership philosophy and leadership mindset. Great leaders also understand that organizational energy, workplace synergy and end results are best attained when ambitious people with different backgrounds and thinking preferences are allowed to perform work together in a safe and supportive environment.

Great leaders know how to create such successful and supportive climates by applying the skills of adaptability, motivation, coaching, focus, collaboration, decision-making, communications, and skill development to both themselves and the people they lead.

Our preferred definition of leadership is: "leadership is the art of achieving progress through the involvement and actions of others."

Great leaders focus on four critical areas to increase employee engagement and drive performance results:

1. Giving team members a sense of purpose and a compelling context for committing to buy-in.

2. Granting team members appropriate levels of autonomy.

3. Showing empathy to team members by understanding the emotions and feelings they are going through, particularly during times of change.

4. Creating a safe environment where mistakes are tolerated (and learned from) and where accountability is fair and unbiased.

These four critical areas help leaders leverage the emotions of passion, enthusiasm, self-satisfaction, trust, and loyalty to drive creativity, thinking, innovation, energy, and buy-in to strategies, tactics and activities in pursuit of clearly stated goals and objectives.

Leaders also have to inspire confidence in the organization and its sustainable future.

With a personal leadership philosophy and a strong leadership mindset — combined with a purposeful set of leadership behaviors — you can develop into a leader of which you will be proud.

For, in the most oft-quoted Yoda saying of all: "Do or do not. There is no try."

## Leading Teams and People

Great leaders know that sustainable, repeatable, replicable success results from collaborative, collective and engaged efforts. This is why great leaders concentrate on the people side of success, including motivation, team building, interpersonal skills of team members, and group recognition and group rewards.

When it comes to leading people, leaders have four distinct audiences:

- The teams that report to them.
- Cross-functional teams that they lead.
- Individuals who directly report to them.
- Individuals with whom they work.

For each audience, a different skill set and approach is required. However, there is one common criteria — since they are dealing with individuals, or a collection of individuals, each leadership situation requires an individualized approach suited for the various demeanors, motivational needs and communication preferences of those being led.

This means that great leaders must be flexible in their leadership approach and with the motivational and communication tactics they use.

**Leading Teams**

Leading teams is fraught with peril and numerous opportunities for mistakes, especially by new or inexperienced leaders. This is mostly due to the dynamic nature of teams, including how individuals on a team interact with one another.

Despite these hurdles, the goal is to achieve Gibbs Rule #15: "Always work as team."

The two team leadership concepts I have found most useful are:

1) The Nature of Teams by Dr. Bruce Tuckman

2) The Five Dysfunctions of Teams by Patrick Lencioni

All successful teams progress through the four stages of the Tuckman model. Unsuccessful teams get mired in one of the first three stages. The four stages of the Tuckman model are:

> **Forming** — the initial stage of team development. Personal relationships have not been determined or evolved. Objectives are mostly likely vague or new to the group. Processes and procedures have yet to be established, and individual roles are undefined. In this stage teams familiarize, orientate and define themselves. The climate is comfortable,

the mood generally friendly and group members tend to be on their best behavior.

**Storming** — in this stage multiple ideas start to collide and compete for attention and consideration. This usually results in the first conflicts between individuals or coalitions of team members. Different opinions start to arise challenging the objectives and even the actual problems to be resolved. Individuals start to jostle for assignments, responsibilities and leadership roles. The climate is contentious and may be seen as unproductive, unpleasant and painful to individuals who are conflict adverse. Leaders are often frustrated by what they see as a lack of cooperation. Teams that cannot resolve their issues in this stage either get stuck here or disband.

**Norming** — alignment and general consensus on key issues, roles and responsibilities are seen. The group also decides on its decision-making process and levels of individual authority to act on the group's behalf. Team members are committed to both the process and the agreed upon objectives. The team's goal starts to take priority over individual objectives and agendas. The climate is less contentious, which is both good (for relationships) and bad (for generating out-of-the-box thinking and ensuring that tough and controversial topics are actually tabled). As things are now working well, leaders often make the mistake of reducing their engagement with the team in order to focus on other challenges and opportunities. This may cause the team to slip back to the storming stage, especially if the team feels abandoned or no longer important.

**Performing** — with trust between team members now in place, the primary focus is on results and relationships. Cooperation, rather than individual competition, becomes the norm. As does shared responsibility for results. Leadership of the team is collectively participatory, and often rotates between individuals depending on the task or challenge at hand. Any dissent or disagreement is centered on ideas, not people or personalities. Teams that reach and remain in the performing stage are often labeled high-performing teams.

This progression is not always a straight sequence through each stage. At any point a team can fall back one or more stages, particularly when a major change event occurs such as a new team member or leader.

One of the biggest mistakes leaders make is to step away when their teams are in the norming stage. Since things are generally working well in the norming stage, leaders see this as an opportune time to reduce their engagement with the team and move on to something else. This often causes problems and, in many cases, results in the team slipping back into storming phase behaviors.

Strong leadership is still required until the team is fully entrenched in the performing stage. It is only at this point that the leader can step away and let the team manage itself.

Cohesive teams break down for many reasons. Almost all of these causes are covered and explained in Lencioni's Five Dysfunctions of a Team:

    Dysfunction #1: Absence of Trust

    Dysfunction #2: Fear of Conflict

    Dysfunction #3: Lack of Commitment

    Dysfunction #4: Avoidance of Accountability

    Dysfunction #5: Inattention to Results

Preventing these five team dysfunctions is a primary concern of a great leader. This often requires an unbiased assessment of individual actions and motives, as well as keen eyes and ears for the various early warning signals.

Not all groups of individuals comprise a true team. Even when managers talk about "my team" often this is really only a group of individuals performing similar, but not necessarily inter-related work who all happen to report to the same individual.

As I have often said in my leadership development programs: "A team is not a group of people who work together. A team is a group of people working together towards a shared outcome who trust and respect each other."

Trust and respect between team members, and between the team leader and team members, is critical. Perhaps this is why one version of Gibbs Rule #1 goes: "Never screw over your partner." This rule means that the relationship between investigative partners is more important than the outcome of any particular case. The same applies in the real world: relationships and trust between team members far outweighs immediate results. After all, if the trust is gone, future collaboration and working partnerships will simply not happen.

Great leaders excel at creating and maintaining high-performing, cohesive teams, which are characterized by:

- Utilization of the diverse skills, knowledge and experience of all team members.

- Alignment around mutually agreed upon common objectives and goals.

- Robust conversations and debates on critical issues that lead to high-quality decisions.

- Individual and group accountability.

- Learning from mistakes.

- Fixing problems by looking for solutions, not blame.

## Leading People

Most managers and leaders think that leading people is only about attaining desired performance results and helping people cope with, accept and implement change.

I would argue that great leaders accomplish great results and implement change by focusing on employee engagement. Great leaders know full well that performance results and change implementation are actually best derived by the engagement and motivation of team members.

For years managers were taught that employees can be motivated through a mixture of rewards and punishment. I am not sure how true this ever was, but it certainly has about zero validity today.

In late 2013, the Deloitte Center for the Edge surveyed approximately 3000 workers in the U.S. across 15 industries. The results showed that almost 88% of those surveyed do not contribute to their full potential in their jobs because they do not have passion for their work. That leaves just 12% of the U.S. workforce possessing what Deloitte calls "the attributes of worker passion."

Employee engagement should be a critical concern of all leaders today, but apparently it is not. I say this because Gallup has been monitoring employee engagement around the world for years, and the needle hardly ever moves. Either few leaders are taking employee disengagement seriously, or their actions are ineffective.

In the latest Gallup State of the Global Workforce study (2013), the prevalence of disengagement in the workforce is astonishing. The data shows that 87% of employees worldwide are not engaged at work. Additionally, actively disengaged employees outnumber engaged employees by nearly 2 to 1.

The data for the U.S. is very similar to the worldwide figures, with results from the 2014 Gallop Survey in the U.S. showing

68.5% of employees are not engaged and only 31.5% being engaged.

The cost of employee disengagement are phenomenal. According to Gallup, companies with highly engaged workforces outperform their peers by 147% in earnings per share. These companies also realize on average:

- 41% fewer quality defects.
- 48% fewer safety incidents.
- 28% less shrinkage (employee theft or wastage).
- 65% less turnover (in low turnover organizations).
- 25% less turnover (in high turnover organizations).
- 37% less absenteeism.

As the Gallup survey shows, there are some hefty benefits and savings to be gained from having a highly engaged workforce.

**Driving Participation**
It is the leader's responsibility to drive participation of the people she or he leads.

Employee engagement is not rocket science. But it does require placing an organization-wide focus on leading people to achieve results over an emphasis on getting things done and improving productivity ratios.

In fact, Mark Barros, in his article *What Your Employees Really Want* (*Inc.*, October 2013), simplifies how to increase employee engagement into three categories of things motivated employees deeply want:

1) A sense of purpose / to know they are contributors.

2) Some amount of autonomy.

3) Empathy from their supervisors / leaders.

The great leaders I have known excelled in all three of these areas. I would add a fourth criteria to the list from Mr. Barros: a safe environment where mistakes are tolerated (and learned from) and where accountability is fair and unbiased.

Some of the best ways to motivate today's workforce are:

- Eliminate long-standing stupid rules, procedures and processes no longer appropriate for today's workforce.

- Be flexible in how you lead individuals and team members.

- Provide on-going and timely feedback to all team members.

- Never act like you are superior or better than your team members simply because you are the boss or the designated leader.

There are two best practices for obtaining employee participation. Both are easy to implement, though one has a greater degree of risk involved (but also a higher potential payback as well).

The first method helps to get introverts and naturally shy people involved in discussions. I first witnessed this practice by the then chairman of the Singapore Tourism Promotion Board when I participated on various volunteer committees of STPB when working and living in Singapore. Before he concluded any meeting, this leader would go around the table and ask each person, individually and by name, if they had any thoughts or ideas to add to the discussions held in that meeting. He did this in an open and receptive manner, and purposely did not call on only those who had not participated in the discussion. He would also thank each person who took the opportunity to speak out.

This process, done in a safe and friendly manner, invariably elicited ideas and comments from even the quietest person in the room. And even when it didn't, the process showed everyone that these discussions were to be open and highly participatory, something not normally found in the typical hierarchical Asian government statutory board at the time.

The second method of increasing participation and engagement of team members is to delegate the lead on a project. Everyone on the project team, including the boss, must follow the lead of the project leader.

Obviously, the person being delegated to suddenly becomes highly participatory. But so do their colleagues and co-workers, who know that they will need this person's participation whenever they are likewise given an opportunity to lead.

Special Agent Gibbs even has a rule on this — Rule 38 — which goes "Your case, your lead." In at least two episodes of NCIS Gibbs has passed the leadership baton to one of his team members, and then quickly fallen in line to do whatever is requested by the new case leader.

In doing so, not only does Gibbs increase participation by all members of his team, but he also demonstrates through action the importance of following the led and directions of the leader (a leadership based on assignment, not job title or organizational rank).

We will discuss more about participation, and how this leads to team member buy-in, in chapter five on Leading For Results. But first let's delve into an exploration of why great leaders excel at leading people development.

## Leading People Development

Here is a revealing exercise that I run in my leadership development programs and one-on-one coaching sessions. If you would like to participate, grab a writing instrument and a piece of paper.

The exercise is to answer these three questions while thinking about a typical two-week period at work:

1) What percentage of your time is spent attending meetings, participating on conference calls, or reading / responding / deleting / sending emails?

2) What percentage of your time is spent reviewing work progress or results (this includes reading / reviewing documents or reports), or on generating reports or presentations on work progress or results?

3) What percentage of your time is spent doing Individual Contributor work?

Add up the three figures. Is the total higher than 80%? Higher than 90%?

Subtract the total from 100. That's the percent of time remaining in your typical work life for developing your people.

For many leaders, especially mid-level leaders and supervisors, people development time is less than 15%. Yet people development is (or should be) one of the key priorities for all leaders, as it is one of the most important drivers of sustainable success for any organization.

In fact, I would suggest that people development should be the single most important priority for all leaders. After all, if a leader is one who achieves progress through the involvement and actions of others, then greater progress will be made when the people being led are constantly being developed and improved.

Additionally, great leaders know that people development can be a highly leveraged catalyst for individuals as well as for the organization. That is why the best leadership talent is bringing out the talent in others.

**Developing People and Teams**
Not surprisingly, the latest FORTUNE 100 Best Companies to Work For annual study (2016) shows that the best companies are committed to employee development. In fact, the companies on this list devote an average of 73 hours per annum toward developing salaried employees. They also invest an average of 58 hours per year for the development of their hourly workers.

A focus on people development differentiates the best companies to work for from all others. A focus on people development is also one of the actions that differentiates great leaders from good leaders.

Everyone on your team has talents that can be improved. These can be the functional skills needed to perform their jobs, or the interpersonal skills required to get work done with others. Great leaders ensure that all members of their teams receive on-going development, both formally and informally. As Special Agent Gibbs says, "You don't waste good."

This is nothing new, though a focus by leaders on developing the skills of one's people has been misplaced in recent decades by an over emphasis on quarterly profits and other short-term performance measurements. For, as John Quincy Adams noted centuries ago, "If your actions inspire others to dream more, learn more, do more, and become more, you are a leader."

So how do you go about being an excellent leader of people development?

First, have an understanding that developing the skills of your team members is your responsibility as a leader. Your organization's Human Resources and Talent Development departments are resources for you to use in this endeavor. But it is your responsibility to ensure the continuous development of your team members and yourself, not theirs.

Speaking of which, it is also important to understand that your own continuous development as a leader is also your responsibility (as well as your boss's). We will delve into the subject of your personal leadership development momentarily.

There are so many resources, both free and paid, on leadership and skill development available through the Internet (articles, videos, book excerpts, and leadership quotations) that there is no valid excuse for any leader to not be constantly upgrading their leadership, motivational, communication, collaboration, coaching, and people development skills. I have a list of highly recommended leadership resources on our company website at www.CalienteLeadership.com.

**Tools for People Development**
There are six main methodologies for leading people development, including three that come under the traditional heading of training. These six methods are:

    1) Feedback

    2) Coaching

    3) Delegation

4) On-the-job training

5) Team training

6) Formal classroom training

The 70-20-10 Model for Learning and Development states that individuals obtain 70% of their work-related knowledge from job-related experiences, 20% from interactions with others and 10% from formal education events such as training programs.

Hence, as a leader of people, you should focus your team member development efforts, for both teams and individuals, on the first five methods above. Your Human Resource and Talent Development colleagues should take the lead only on formal training events, which include both classroom and virtual training programs.

Yoda is the member of our leadership brain trust who places the most emphasis on the leader's role in people development. A fundamental part of Yoda's leadership mindset is seen when he says, "Always pass on what you have learned."

Of course, Yoda sees himself as a great teacher. In fact, teaching and coaching are core components of his essence throughout his appearances in the *Star Wars* series. He even speaks to this: "You think Yoda stops teaching just because his student does not want to learn? A teacher Yoda is. Yoda teaches like drunkards drink, like killers kill."

Feedback is a specialized form of coaching, one with many which managers and leaders struggle. Part of the reason for this is that feedback has been taught as either positive or negative, with the latter difficult to deliver.

To make the delivery of negative feedback easier, managers and leaders have for years been taught the "sandwich model," in which negative feedback is sandwiched between so-called positive feedback statements.

This process really does not work. As soon as you give someone a piece of positive feedback, they wait for the "but..." to appear. Telling someone "they have done something well, but..." negates the positive impact of the opening words.

When giving feedback your intention should be to help someone build competency and/or confidence in their abilities by helping them determine how to change or improve performance. Basically your intention when giving feedback should be to help someone learn and develop.

Hence, if your intention is to help someone improve, learn or develop how could any feedback be perceived as negative? All leaders should dump the phrases "positive feedback" and "negative feedback" from their terminology. Instead, replace these with the phrases "reinforcing feedback" and "developmental feedback."

Use reinforcing feedback when you want to reinforce performance or behavior that is producing desired results and outcomes. Your goal here is recognition of what a person is doing well in order to encourage and motivate them to continue doing so more frequently or in other relevant situations. This not only improves the likelihood of such performance or behavior being repeated, it also builds confidence in the person receiving such feedback.

Use developmental feedback when there is a need to provide corrective instructions or to help someone determine how to change or improve their performance. Again, it is given with the intention of helping that person learn and develop, as well as shaping desired behavior and increasing the likelihood that future performance will be improved.

All feedback should be delivered in an on-going, timely and non-judgmental manner. It also needs to be specific, descriptive, detailed, actionable, and future focused. You are not looking for ownership of blame here or excuses. You are looking for ways to improve future performance or to correct unacceptable behavior going forward.

Jack Sparrow obviously knows the power of reinforcing feedback: "Well done mates. I knew you had it in you. Now, come back in eight minutes and we'll do it all over again, eh?" Such feedback is undoubtedly designed to motivate his crew to return to a hard task with greater confidence and determination. Who knew that people development via reinforcing feedback was the pirate way?

**Leading Self Development**

No leader should wait around for their manager to tell them how to develop as a leader. As April Arnzen, Vice President of Human Resources at Micron Technology, tells her leaders throughout this Fortune 500 organization, "Don't ever wait around for someone else to tell you how to develop yourself." That's sage advice for leaders at any level of any organization.

You could do a whole lot worse than using Yoda as your personal leadership development coach. His numerous insightful comments to Luke Skywalker and others are worthy of being said to any leader, including yourself.

For instance, Yoda's comment that "Many of the truths that we cling to depend on our point of view," is spot on. Unfortunately too many leaders are unaware of the origins of the points of view they cling to. That is why having an acute understanding of your own leadership philosophy and mindset is critical (refer to chapter two).

Constantly thinking about and exploring the foundation of your leadership philosophy and mindset is a core component of your on-going leadership development journey.

Chances are you already know what leadership gaps you have, as well as what your leadership strengths are. The key to leveraging your strengths is through consistent behavior and actions. Purposeful action, based on your core leadership beliefs, prevents the handling of every situation you evaluate in an inconsistent, case-by-case manner.

Your leadership strengths can also be used to minimize or close any leadership skill gaps you have. Or at least buy you time to eliminate these gaps through coaching from others, your own reading and video research, or a formal classroom session. Closing your leadership skill gaps is unlikely to be difficult for, as Master Coach Yoda points out, "Already know you that which you need."

Two other quotes from Yoda re-assure us that we all constantly have more to learn (which is a good thing!):

> *"Ready are you? What know you of ready? For eight hundred years have I trained Jedi. My own comment will I keep on who is to be trained. A Jedi must have the deepest commitment, the most serious mind."*

> *"Much to learn you still have...my old Padawan...this is just the beginning!"*

My last advice is to approach your leadership development and learning journey with an open mind. Great leadership is an art, based on a core set of skills and behaviors you can learn. We will give Yoda the last word on how to learn the art of great leadership:

> *"You must unlearn what you have learned."*

> *"Truly wonderful the mind of a child is."*

## Leading For Results

Great leaders drive results by focusing on four skills and behaviors:

- Communicating as a leader.
- Ensuring individual and team accountability.
- Developing clear and concise strategy statements.
- Leveraging cross-functional and cross-cultural collaboration.

One of our core leadership beliefs is that leaders can be found at all levels of an organization. Leadership is not something confined to the upper ranks of management or the top tiers of an organization chart.

Likewise, strategy is not something done only at the corporate or strategic business unit level. Any leader can have a strategy, such as:

A customer retention strategy.

A service quality strategy.

An innovation strategy.

A new product strategy.

A cost-reduction strategy.

A leadership development strategy.

A team development strategy.

However, setting a strategy or a vision for your work group is never sufficient in itself. Far too many strategies fail to achieve their intended outcomes. I'll share with you later in this chapter some of the main reasons why strategic plans fail.

## Setting Strategic Direction

A strategy is simply a vision of going from a current situation to a desired state, complete with actionable plans and identified resources. But while this may sound simple, in reality most strategies are anything but simple. In addition, as Jedi Master Yoda teaches us, "Difficult to see. Always in motion is the future."

When created in the upper echelons of organizations, strategies tend to be convoluted, cross-functional, big picture in scope, and longer term in outlook and completion tenure. When created at the coalface of operations, strategies tend to be tactical and short-term in nature and usually aimed at solving a single specific problem or challenge.

Mid-level leaders are often tasked with taking strategies developed above and creating executional strategies, tactics and plans to accomplish the assigned goals and objectives. This is why I often refer to mid-level leaders as "the glue between strategy and execution."

At all levels strategies must provide a clear road map for where the leader wants the organization or team to go, the resources available to get there, and the reasons why it is important to move in the stated direction and toward the desired outcome.

It is the leader's responsibility to determine the destination and desired state for which the strategy and action plans will be designed. You may involve others in the formulation of your strategies, but my advice is to keep such groups small and highly focused. Too much involvement and participation of others at the strategy development stage can cause unnecessary delays, a slowed process and even paralysis by analysis. As a leader you must drive this process expeditiously so that, in the words of our pirate leader Sparrow, "Where we want to go, we'll go."

If it takes too long to develop a strategy, or to execute it, the desired results may be missed. Those who hesitate often lose out to more nimble and swifter competitors. As Jack Sparrow told one hesitant leader, "If you were waiting for the opportune moment, that was it." That is not something you want your bosses, or even your team members, telling you.

Remember any strategy is a living thing. You can course correct or make modifications in execution any time you sense you and your team have gone off track. As long as you keep the final destination and the desired results in mind, changes in execution are okay. It's like sailing, you have to tack and change your sail configuration whenever the wind changes.

On the other hand, do not lead by the seat of your pants. Great leaders are those with strategies, execution plans and resources in hand. Capt'n Jack Sparrow may get way with simply responding to each situation he faces, but that's Hollywood. It doesn't work in real life, at least not frequently nor for long.

One last point. In one of the *Pirates of the* Caribbean movies, Theodore Graves says to Cutler Beckett about Sparrow, "Do you think he plans it all out, or makes it up as he goes along?" Again, this is not something you want your bosses, or your team members, asking about you.

Rather, have them say about your strategies what Sparrow noted about a particular plan under discussion, "This is either madness or brilliance. It's remarkable how often the two coincide."

### Why Strategic Plans Fail
Research shows that over 70% of all change initiatives worldwide fail to achieve their intended results. Surprisingly, this figure has remained fairly constant for several decades.

Why are organizations so poor at implementing strategic plans?

One key reason, according to Bridges Business Consulting International, is that "leadership teams habitually underestimate the implementation challenge and what is involved." In our estimation, this really goes back to the leadership team creating the executional "hows" rather than involving the frontline implementers in helping to craft the executional tactics and plans.

Too often the post mortems on failed strategies reveal these causes:

- Strategy is often set by those who do not have to execute it.

- Strategy is frequently set by those who do not understand how to execute it.

- Strategies are often overly optimistic on what is required to execute successfully.

- Leaders want strategies executed immediately, or as quickly as possible, without understanding the ramifications of expedited deadlines.

- Leaders often fall in love with their own ideas without fully understanding what it takes to implement those ideas.

As you can see, it is often the way leaders approach problems, and how they determine the solution required, that often cause strategic plans to go astray. As you face your next big challenge as a leader, you may want to keep this observation from Capt'n Jack Sparrow in mind, "The problem is not the problem. The problem is your attitude about the problem."

Be sure that your attitude and your perspective about future problems do not impact the strategies and solutions you develop. That is an important tip for all leaders.

There are many other reasons why strategic plans fail. Here are 10 of the most prominent ones:

1) Unrealistic goals.

2) Lack of focus and resources.

3) Plans that are overly complex.

4) Financial estimates that are significantly inaccurate (and usually over optimistic).

5) Plans based on insufficient data.

6) Inflexible or undefined team roles and responsibilities (often leading to confusion, inaction or wrong steps).

7) Staffing requirements not fully understood.

8) Project scope is inflexible with no room to meet changing conditions.

9) Leaders believe the hardest part is creating the strategy, when in fact implementation is the hardest part.

10) Leaders do not communicate clearly and frequently.

Great leaders will provide an overview of how to achieve the strategic objectives, but leave the details of the "how" to those executing the strategy. Average leaders, on the other hand, are more likely to develop and include the details of execution in their strategy plans, forcing the execution teams to follow a designated path. This methodology has a lower degree of successful execution than the process used by great leaders.

Of course, the worst leaders are those who keep their heads down and hope that any new strategies or changes announced by their own leaders are merely passing fads or temporary "hot buttons of the month" that will fade into oblivion once the senior leadership team casts their collective eyes on another opportunity or challenge. We might call this the

Capt'n Jack Sparrow approach, as our famed pirate advises, "Close your eyes and pretend it's all a bad dream. That's how I get by."

Here is another piece of advice from Captain Sparrow to keep in mind when developing future strategies, "It's not the destination so much as the journey, they say." One way to make the journey exciting, relatable and positively anticipatory for your team members, colleagues and others is through well written Strategy Statements.

**Strategy Statements**
When team members are handed a strategy that they do not fully understand, or for which the underlying reasons are not clear or known, they typically become:

- Confused
- Scared
- Uncertain
- Afraid to act
- Uncommitted
- Withholders of buy-in
- Unwilling to do more than exactly what they are told to do

The best way to overcome such confusion and reluctance is through a well-crafted Strategy Statement. This is a short description of a strategy that provides an overview of the strategy, the expected benefits when successfully achieved and a compelling context for why it should be supported.

There are five components to a well-designed Strategy Statement:

1) It is concise and clear.

2) It identifies what success looks like.

3) It provides a compelling context for why team members (at all levels) should support the strategy and be engaged in executing it.

4) It should be easily communicated by all team members.

5) It leads to buy-in at all levels.

The most important key to an excellent Strategy Statement is the compelling context. The compelling context for the strategy must be something that drives discretionary energy from the team members executing the strategy. It's this discretionary energy (physical, emotional and mental energies) that differentiates a commitment to a strategy and one that creates a higher level of buy-in.

In essence a good Strategy Statement provides a clear line of sight for every team member to understand how their individual contributions and actions impact both team and organizational results. It also provides them with a compelling and persuasive reason that drives their involvement, dedication and determination in execution of the plan.

It goes without saying that, as a leader, you need to believe in both your strategy and your strategy statements. Your team members will sniff out any hesitation or uncertainty you have.

How important is your personal belief to success? Perhaps Capt'n Jack Sparrow proffers the best advice on this: "I wonder...does it work because it works, or because you believe it works?"

Well, if the compelling context is meaningful to both you and your team members, then it is highly likely you will believe in the strategy and the direction. And if you believe, you have a better chance of attaining your goals, or at least getting pretty close to them.

Clear and concise are also keys to a good Strategy Statement. Keep the wording simple and straight-forward, and easily repeatable. And at all costs avoid this kind of confusing Strategy Statement that comes from our pirate leader Capt'n Jack Sparrow:

> *"If we don't have the key, we can't open whatever it is we don't have that it unlocks. So what purpose would be served in finding whatever needed to be unlocked, which we don't have, without first having found the key what unlocks it?"*

Sparrow certainly knows what the right strategy should be (i.e. find the key before finding the treasure chest), but his message is confusing, is not easy to repeat, and definitely lacks a compelling context.

## Collaboration

Collaboration between individuals, departments, work groups, colleagues, outside contractors, and even between leaders, is essential in today's world.

Hence, leaders are also accountable for ensuring that collaboration takes place between all team members and work groups, as well as between themselves and others.

Collaboration means working together to attain a shared outcome. The key word here is shared.

Collaboration is not about getting others to help achieve your own goals or objectives. There must be benefits to both parties (or to all parties when multi-group collaboration is necessary), though these benefits need not be equal in size, stature or importance.

Also, collaboration does not mean compromise. One party making a compromise does not equate to collaboration. There is a huge difference between asking someone to compromise and asking them to collaborate.

Successful collaboration comes from a strong mixture of three factors:

- Shared goals and outcomes.
- Influence skills.
- Handing collaboration conflict.

Shared goals and outcomes, of course, is part of the very definition of collaboration. The other two factors are leadership skills that need to be learned and honed.

Collaboration works best when there are "big picture" results for customers and the organization. Conflict often ensues when the perceived results overly benefit either customers or the organization. The same is true when a collaboration project on internal processes, policies or procedures greatly favors one part of the organization over another or all others.

Interestingly, it is actually easier for siloed members of an organization to collaborate in times of major stress or in a crises situation. This is because internal barriers and silos come crashing down when an "all hands on deck" situation occurs. Sadly, people tend to go back to their old non-collaborative ways once the crises or urgency is over.

Unfortunately, the silo mentality and the various rewards / recognition systems in most organizations often prevent routine collaboration between team members and peers from happening. Very few organizations rank their team members on their ability to collaborate (despite this being a critical success skill). Likewise, few individual performance goals used in annual performance reviews are based on collaborative results or outcomes.

When such systemic hurdles are in place, it is up to leaders (at all levels) to pro-actively engage in collaboration for the good of their teams, the organization as a whole, or even themselves. Doing so is the hallmark of a great leader, even when the results may not directly impact promotion and bonuses. Doing so will, however, impact results and how the leader is perceived by team members, direct reports and peers.

# Ensuring Accountability

When leaders talk about ensuring accountability they are usually referring to concepts such as holding people accountable for results.

Good leaders take this a step further by emphasizing that accountability is about more than just results. They hold both themselves and others accountable for the decisions and options producing the results, as well as for the actual outcomes. A good leader will also hold herself or himself accountable for utilizing the right level of delegation when appropriately empowering team members.

Great leaders also have a bigger organizational perspective, thus holding themselves and others accountable for how their decisions and actions impact other departments and business units as well as customers and business partners.

Great leaders also go even further by holding themselves and other leaders accountable for their leadership behaviors, actions and for making ethical decisions. I call this Leadership Accountability.

**Leadership Accountability**
At the heart of Leadership Accountability is trust.

Trust is more than the leader being held accountable for doing what they say they will do. Trust also means the leader will make decisions based on what is best for the entire organization, its customers and the world we live in.

Such trust means that personal and departmental agendas are put aside for the greater good and sustainable health of the organization.

Great leaders build trust through transparency and honesty. They are willing to explain the reasons behind decisions. They are also wiling to acknowledge when they do not know the answer or solution to a problem.

Long gone are the days when leaders should never exhibit weakness or vulnerability in front of their team members. Doing so does not cause staff and direct reports to question or doubt your leadership skills. It causes them to see you as human, and as someone struggling with some of the same issues and concerns they are. It is archaic and utter nonsense to think otherwise.

Despite his control and command leadership style, even Special Agent Gibbs is not afraid to admit when he doesn't know something, is unsure of a situation or even when he is wrong. Not surprisingly, this leadership teacher has rules for all such situations:

> When you need help, ask. (Rule 28)

> Sometimes you're wrong. (Rule 51)

Gibbs also holds himself as accountable for his own actions as he does for his team members. Rule 45, which he invokes upon both himself and various team members, is very clear about this: "Clean up the mess that you make."

Without a doubt leaders need to be strong and exhibit resilience, especially during a crisis situation or in particularly difficult and trying times. Such exhibition of strength and displays of resilience will be appreciated and admired by your team members when you and your team are facing enormous challenges and demanding situations.

However, there are appropriate situations and times when, in a positive and forthcoming way, and with the right audience, leaders can admit their vulnerabilities, blind spots, uncertainties, and weaknesses.

In doing so, great leaders become trusted by their followers. Such trust enables followers and other team members to be more willing to raise problems and concerns with their leaders, allowing problems to be dealt with sooner when they are more manageable.

Without trust, no aspect of your leadership philosophy or leadership mindset matters. Without trust your leadership philosophy, mindset and beliefs are simply invalid and unlikely to be accepted by others.

Every leader makes mistakes. Great leaders readily acknowledge their errors and mistakes. And not just to themselves! They own up and admit slipups, blunders, incorrect decisions, miscalculations, and poor leadership behavior to their colleagues, peers and direct reports. Average leaders tend to ignore, brush over or cover up their occasional mistakes, often in the hopes that nobody has noticed. Believe me, they have!

Here are the types of mistakes that leaders make that break the bonds of trust:

- Showing favoritism to one or more team members.

- Withholding information on purpose to keep others, particularly peers, out of the loop or misinformed.

- Showing up unannounced at a meeting being led by a direct report.

- Taking credit for the work of your team without sharing the credit.

- Giving feedback in anger.

- Gossiping or spreading knowingly false stories about colleagues.

- Demanding someone do something simply because you're the boss.

- Not recognizing efforts of team members and considering extra efforts to merely be "part of the job requirement."

- Frequently missing or being late to meetings with team members simply because you're the (very busy) boss, thus not respecting their time, their work loads and their commitments to others.

- Not keeping promises and commitments.

- Making vague, general promises and commitments that you know team members perceive as more rock solid, especially when it concerns their career advancement opportunities.

All of these are easy mistakes to make in the hustle and bustle of the day. But while they may seem like minor infractions, each is a trust buster; especially when they become frequent leadership behaviors.

Great leadership is a mixture of vulnerability, humility, self-confidence, forgiveness, ethical judgment, and a personal code upon which to based leadership behaviors and actions.

It takes all this, and more, to consistently hold yourself and others accountable for all leadership behaviors, actions and decisions.

When Leadership Accountability is absent, as we have seen at Volkswagen, Enron, HSBC, the U.S. Veterans Administration, and other organizations, devastating disasters and ethical crises often arise. In some instances, neither the brand nor the organization recovers from Leadership Accountability lapses.

**Advocating For What Is Right**
Senior leaders and executives often realize that they are not in the best position to identify and know all the challenges involved in strategy execution. Unfortunately too many leaders have mindsets and fears of inadequacies that prevent them readily admitting this. As such they do not solicit ideas and inputs from others, nor do they appear willingly receptive of unsolicited ideas and inputs.

As a result, in far too many organizations there is a culture of reluctance within the lower leadership ranks to raise concerns and red flags with more senior colleagues or more experienced team members. This is even more prevalent when team members are from hierarchical cultures such as those found in North Asia, China, parts of Latin America, and Eastern Europe.

Leaders can only change this culture of reluctance by being seen as open to suggestions, questions and even push-back by their followers and peers. Only a "walk the talk" solution will result in the desired culture change, and it will not happen overnight.

Great leaders devote a significant amount of energy and time to clarifying and understanding the perspectives, ideas, concerns, and questions of others (particularly of those that they lead). Additionally, great leaders do not see clarification questions from team members, peers or others as a sign of push-back or dissention. In fact, they appreciate such questions and inputs, knowing full well that open and honest dialogues are a key builder of trust.

Likewise, great leaders will also demonstrate confidence and courage when providing feedback to their own bosses and other senior leaders. They also assert their right to express their viewpoints, concerns and questions in a professional manner.

This is particularly important for mid-level leaders tasked with implementing the strategies from above. Mid-level leaders need to be stronger advocates for advising senior leaders what is required to successfully implement a strategic plan. Otherwise, as seen in the previous chapter, strategic plans are more likely to fail to meet stated objectives and results.

Admittedly, advocating for what is right is not always easy. This is especially true when trust, openness and honesty have not been mutually established between leaders operating at different levels within an organization. However, it is not impossible to do so, particularly if the following seven-step model for advocating for what is right is followed:

1) Base your argument or position on facts.

2) Name your sources (unless these are strictly confidential).

3) Challenge information presented to you, especially if such information is unsourced or undocumented. Remember, if it is documented or sourced, be sure to challenge the information, not the source.

4) Control your boiling point by exercising self control. You know what angers you, so prepare yourself not to be agitated. The next step also helps with this.

5) Ignore statements without merit. Examples are "you guys in marketing always back the customer over

operatons," or "people in R&D never understand the many manufacturing challenges we face."

6) Focus on the big picture and shared outcomes.

7) Incorporate the best points from others and restate your position (revised or not).

**Corporate Social Accountability**
Let's start with a basic premise: every organization, and in fact every individual, has the obligation to make the world a better place for our children and grandchildren to inherit.

It's that simple.

It is also a huge responsibility.

From a corporate perspective, this is augmented by short-term responsibilities to four specific sets of stakeholders: customers, employees, shareholders, and the communities in which the organization operates.

Much like the racial segregation and marriage equality laws that have evolved in recent decades, the moral compass on corporate responsibility continues to evolve.

This progression is created by a combination of societal pressures, changing social values and mores, and an increasingly more knowledgeable and frustrated global population. Added to this combustible mix is an increasingly active citizenry that does not hesitate to punish or correct organizations deemed to be outside the boundaries of proper corporate citizenship.

We even see organizations themselves now taking stands against other organizations negatively impacting the world, for instance:

- Starbucks committing to 100% ethically sourced coffee and tea in a global program that aims to positively impact the lives and livelihoods of farmers and their communities.

- Intel committing to use minerals from "conflict-free" sources in the Congo so that their purchases of such minerals do not fund the militant violence and human-rights atrocities in the Democratic Republic of the Congo.

- Grocery chain NTUC FairPrice in Singapore removing products from its shelves made by the company suspected of being involved in the burning of forests in Indonesia which caused an unhealthy smoke haze to descend upon Singapore for weeks.

There can be little doubt, therefore, that Corporate Responsibility is one of the pillars of sustainable success for any organization or corporate entity.

The key word here is sustainable.

Many organizations pay public and internal lip service to the concept of Corporate Social Responsibility. And many get away with this for years and years. But if they do wrong, at some point they will get caught and then disaster strikes.

Witness the recent events surrounding the Volkswagen saga, and the direct impact on three of its four key constituents.

First, employees. Volkswagen employs over 580,000 people worldwide. Let's assume that its diesel engine cars would not have met EPA emission standards in the USA without the company resorting to the cheating it engaged in. That obviously would have resulted in reduced sales, and probably led to a reduced workforce.

So can cheating be condoned when it is perceived to be in the best interest of employees and shareholders?

Such a mentality treats the concept of "best interest" on a short-term thinking basis. And all it does is postpone the inevitable. Workers who would have been fired if car sales declined are now likely to be laid off as the impact of this scandal cascades.

The same goes for shareholders. Short-term holders of shares in Volkswagen benefitted over the seven years while this cheating was being perpetuated. When this saga first unfolded, the share price of Volkswagen was down 40% within just a few weeks. So while one set of shareholders may have benefitted (temporarily), the entire shareholder base is now negatively and massively impacted. One can only hope that this latter group includes all those involved in executing and covering up this duplicitous scandal.

How important is Corporate Responsibility to consumers?

The Edelman goodpurpose™ Consumer Study of 6,000 people in 10 countries showed that an increasing number of people are spending on brands that have a social purpose, despite the prolonged stagnant or slow growth in global economies.

In this study, 57% of respondents globally said a company or brand has earned their business because it has been doing its part to support good causes. Most interestingly, the countries reporting the highest level of such consumer support were in the world's two most populous nations — China (85%) and India (84%).

Two-thirds (67%) globally also reported they would switch brands if another brand of similar quality supported a good cause. This means that a corporation's or brand's identification with supporting social causes would be a key differentiator between brands with similar features and attributes.

As Mitch Markson, Edelman's Chief Executive Officer, stated when these survey results were released, "People are demanding social purpose, and brands are recognizing it as an area where they can differentiate themselves, not only to meet government compliance requirements, but also to build brand equity."

In a sign of hope for the world that our children will inherit, the vast majority (87%) of respondents to this survey globally agreed it was their duty to contribute to a better society and environment and 82% felt they can personally make a difference. But here is the number most important to corporate leaders: 83% are willing to change their own consumption habits to help make tomorrow's world a better place.

The Edelman study also revealed that 70% of consumers felt their ability to make monetary financial contributions to community causes had been limited or reduced by the global recession; many had instead given more time in support of good causes because they had not been able to contribute as much financially as in the past.

While the Edelman survey clearly reveals that social purpose has become increasingly important to a brand's success, the report's findings also state, "a brand purpose must be authentic and true to the core values of the brand itself and brands must look beyond traditional corporate social responsibility programs in which they simply donate money to a good cause."

As the survey notes, 66% of the respondents in these 10 countries no longer believe it is good enough for corporations and brands to merely give money away to charitable causes. The belief now is that, to be authentic, corporations and brands must truly integrate good causes into their day-to-day business activities, as well as into their internal processes and procedures.

In another Edelman survey, called the Trust Barometer, 80% of the more than 33,000 people surveyed worldwide said they expect businesses to both make money and improve economic and social conditions in their countries. In addition, 67% felt that businesses are too focused on short-term financial gains, while 57% felt that businesses are not focused enough on their long-term impact on society.

This takes the importance of Corporate Responsibility and Corporate Accountability to a new level.

Going back to the Volkswagen saga. Buyers of the Volkswagen and Audi cars that have the dishonest software installed now own vehicles with greatly reduced resale value. They also face the inconvenience of eventually having to bring their cars into a dealership to have the corrected software installed.

Potential customers of Volkswagen are undoubtedly looking elsewhere for their next vehicle purchase. Reduced sales will impact the VW labor force, its car dealership network and even its suppliers of materials and parts.

Volkswagen as a corporate entity — which means both its leadership team as well as every employee with knowledge of these shenanigans — had a responsibility to their customers, fellow employees (and their families), the dealer network owners and employees (and their families), and the owners and employees of all its materials and parts suppliers (and their families).

Volkswagen — meaning its leadership team and the employees with knowledge of this deliberate subterfuge — failed to live up to their collective and individual responsibilities to these stakeholders and their families.

In society, when people do not live up to their collective and individual responsibilities to the community, they are usually jailed, ostracized or outcast.

In the corporate world, such failure to meet the duties of corporate responsibility result in massive loss of value, reputation, market share, and, of course, sustainable success.

# Communicating As A Leader

Communicating is at the heart of leadership. Almost by definition great leaders are great communicators. In fact, I cannot think of any great leaders who were poor communicators.

For many years being great at leadership communication was thought to be a function of using the right words, exhibiting the right passions and delivering one's message in a strong, forceful manner. And while that approach worked pretty well in the old command and control generation of leadership, there is a whole lot more today to being a great communicator.

If your internal communication is not good, and by that we mean clear and concise, then your external communication (either outside your department or outside your organization) will likely end up being overly focused on rationalizing and explaining negative outcomes and events. A leader cannot be muddled and disorganized when communicating within his or her organization and expect to be a clear and focused communicator outside it.

Leaders must take time to clearly communicate with their teams. And this starts with being equally good at two critical communication skills: questioning and listening.

## Questioning Skills

Great leaders ask the right kinds of questions in order to get to the root causes of a problem, or to determine the full scope of a team member's concerns or issues.

They also ask the right questions to ensure that they are getting complete details and the full story of a situation. Great leaders know that too often subordinates are inclined to say what they think the leader wants to hear rather than their own assessment and knowledge of a situation.

Even when all the right questions have been asked and answered, great leaders do their own checking of facts, data and missing information. In doing so, they apply three of the rules from Special Agent Gibbs:

> Don't believe what you're told. Double check. (One version of Rule 3)
>
> Never take anything for granted. (Rule 8)
>
> If you feel like you are being played, you probably are. (Rule 36)

In the episode *Rekindled* Rule 8 above is referred to as "never assume." Either way it is stipulated it is very good advice indeed for leaders.

Gibbs also believes it is important to "don't stop checking and rechecking evidence until you are satisfied." While that is super important for him and his investigative team, it is useful advice for all leaders at all levels.

**Listening Skills**
To start with, great communicators are great listeners. And so are great leaders. In fact, I always tell my leadership development participants that since they each have two ears and one mouth, they should use these proportionately in communicating as a leader. In other words, they will benefit most from listening twice as much as they speak.

I firmly believe that listening is the number one communication skill a leader must have. This is particularly true for new leaders, as the tendency is to think that once one is put into a leadership position it is a requirement to have all the answers and to bark out all the orders. Nothing could be further from the truth.

There is more to listening than simply hearing the words others are saying. Rather, leaders need to develop their active listening skills, which means observing the emotions, feelings, expressions, and body language behind what is being said. It also means acutely listening for what is not being said and for what is intentionally being left out.

Stephen Covey, author of the book *The 7 Habits of Highly Effective People*, identified a key problem in communicating, both professionally and personally. He noted that too many of us "listen with the intent to respond, not with the intent to understand."

Listening with the intent to understand is a crucial skill for leaders. Fortunately it is also one that can be developed and enhanced, through practice and reflection.

### How People Receive and Retain Information

There are three ways human beings absorb and retain information:

> Visually — by what they see.
>
> Orally — by what they hear.
>
> Experientially — by what they experience.

Naturally, all of us absorb and retain information through all three methodologies. But, at the same time, we each have our preferences and strengths for how we receive and retain information.

For instance, some people need to see and read a name in order to remember it. Others are good at remembering names just by hearing them. And others can only remember someone's name when they have actually met the person and thus have something (experience) to associate with that person.

As a communicator, a leader's job is to ensure what is communicated is received, understood and retained. Hence, a leader often needs to change the way he or she delivers their messages, based on the information absorption and retention preferences of their audiences.

**Impact of Frequency on Communications**
Numerous research studies have shown that messages need to be received more than once to be understood.

In fact, the minimum threshold is three to seven times, depending on the complexity of the message. This is why you often see the same commercial two or three times during the same television program (particularly sporting events and movies). Advertisers know that we all need to see their messages multiple times before we start to understand them.

The time interval between receipt of messages will also impact message comprehension and retention. The shorter the interval between messages, the higher likelihood of greater understanding and retention.

This means that leaders need to communicate strategies and action plans several times, especially if either is highly complex or intricate.

Additionally, as leaders you need to remember that you have typically been working on your strategies and action plans for a period of time, usually weeks or months. This means you will have spent hours and hours looking at the pros and cons of your plans and evaluating the various options available.

It is not realistic, however, to expect your team members to immediately understand and accept what you communicate to them after hearing it only once. They need time to digest your messages and go over the key points several times before reaching the same level of understanding and acceptance that you have.

Also, since people have different preferences for how they absorb and retain information, your team members are going to need to hear your communications (orally), see a written version of your communications (visually) and perhaps even experience a test pilot or sample of your strategies and plans (experiential) before full understanding and commitment take place.

Effective leaders are patient and know how to leverage the technique of frequency in their communications. As Yoda advises, "Patience you must have, my young Padawan."

## Motivating Through Communications

Another aspect of communication that leaders must learn is how to truly understand what motivates people. Again, this is a skill that can be learned and then honed through practice and self assessment.

Unfortunately, what motivates people, particularly in the workplace, is not always the most obvious things, such as awards, bonuses or promotions.

For instance, a highly skilled R&D individual contributor might be motivated to work on a team project which could lead to a patent. Or someone in Human Resources might be motivated to lead a project that will produce benefits for a significant number of fellow team members.

One great way to motivate people through communications is to provide each person with a clear line of sight to their role and importance on a task or project. When a leader's communication provides clarity and understanding, and the leader engages in a dialogue that openly discusses the concerns and questions of other team members, then motivation and buy-in are more likely to occur.

A clear line of sight shows team members how they are contributing to the team or business unit, and how the team or business unit in turn is contributing to the success of the organization.

Great leadership communications and behaviors ensure that these four things highly motivated employees want are covered:

1) A sense of purpose and to know they are contributors.

2) Some amount of autonomy.

3) Empathy from their supervisors and leaders.

4) A safe workplace environment to express their questions and concerns and to learn from mistakes.

All of these communication techniques, when used repeatedly in your daily communications with team members, will make you a better leader.

## Great Leadership Is An Art

Great leadership is an art.

It is the art of achieving progress through the involvement and actions of others. This is why great leaders are strong in leading both people and results, while good leaders typically have a leadership focus on either one or the other.

This philosophy of leadership is applicable across all organizations and institutions, including publicly listed companies, non-profit entities, social and community groups, educational institutions, and even government departments and ministries.

You may have noticed that we do not refer to achievement of goals and objectives in this definition. Many factors will impact whether particular goals are achieved or attained. Leadership has the role of ensuring progress towards clearly defined goals and objectives.

The inability to achieve a goal is not necessarily failure. After all, learning from non-achievement of a stated objective is not failure, but rather the gaining of new knowledge. Additionally, even small progress is still progress.

As former U.S. President Ronald Reagan said "The greatest leader is not necessarily the one who does the greatest things. He is the one that gets people to do the greatest things."

Great leaders combine a leadership mindset and written leadership philosophy with strong people leadership skills and a results-oriented focus.

Successful great leaders apply the skills of adaptability, motivation, coaching, focus, collaboration, decision-making, communications, and personal development to both themselves and the people they lead.

Strong leaders also leverage the emotions of passion, enthusiasm, self-satisfaction, trust, and loyalty to drive creativity, thinking, innovation, energy, and buy-in to strategies, tactics, and activities in pursuit of clearly stated goals and objectives.

**The Art of Great Leadership**
It has often been said that "managers do things right while leaders do the right things." There's a great deal of truth in this pithy observation. Especially as our concept of leadership is applied.

Managers should be responsible for ensuring appropriate implementation of policies, procedures, and processes. Great leaders, in addition to determining and communicating direction, are responsible for people leadership and people development. This includes leadership and development of themselves.

The art of great leadership mandates a positive and future-focus mindset. You will not find many successful leaders who are pessimistic. Nor are those focused solely on short-term results (such as quarterly revenue and profit figures) likely to be successful over the long term.

This does not mean leadership requires wearing rose-colored glasses, or having an unrealistic view that all will become right soon.

Rather, the art of great leadership requires a solid grounding in both understanding the reality of any situation, while simultaneously being able to integrate various viewpoints of reality that they and others holds. This means both understanding the status quo and being able to question the underlining nature of the status quo, and how this is perceived and believed by others.

Some leaders are born to lead. Most leaders are created by circumstances, aptitude and an internal willingness or drive to lead others.

The thing is: anyone at any level of an organization can be a great leader.

Great leadership is not something reserved for senior management, business owners, and entrepreneurs. Anyone can be a great leader, if only of themselves. One does not need direct reports or to head a multi-functional team to be a great leader. As such, anyone can implement the art of great leadership and the skills of great leadership.

## Developing As A Leader

The people development aspect of leadership is often overlooked by leaders, especially by those put into leadership positions for the first time, such as new supervisors, frontline managers, and newly appointed sales managers who have been promoted due to high sales performance.

Leaders whose key aim to attract followers are interested in authority, power, status, and control. They drive to make people get things done — usually their way (or the highway). While this often produces wonderful short-term results, it is not a sustainable or replicable leadership methodology. It also tends to lead to employee burnout and high employee attrition rates.

However, all great leaders know that their mission is not to create followers, but to create more good leaders for their organizations. They also know they need to continuously develop themselves. This is why people development, including one's own personal development, is a core component of the art of great leadership.

In one episode of *NCIS*, Agent Timothy McGee (a member of Gibbs's team) says, *"It takes a man to make a man,"* in a letter he pens to his father. I believe this also applies to leadership. It takes a great leader to make a great leader.

For many, particularly new leaders, leadership is a bit like parenting. Our parenting skills come from our own parents and those of our partner. Likewise, many in leadership positions have learned leadership only by observing their own leaders and others around them. Unfortunately, that is not good enough.

The biggest mistake new leaders make is thinking they know everything they need to excel in their new leadership role. However, the skills, knowledge and experiences that create a successful and talented individual contributor are not necessarily transferable to the role of a leader. The truth is, you will never learn everything you need to know to be a great leader. Continuous learning and development is mandatory for continued leadership success.

For instance, you may know how to motivate yourself. But what motivates you is not necessarily what motivates your team members. The same applies to communication preferences. You may prefer delivering your messages orally, but some team members may need to see these in writing for them to understand and retain them. This advice from Jedi

Master Yoda is particularly relevant for new leaders, "You must unlearn what you have learned."

Your development as a leader will also come through experiences, especially difficult ones. As Morgan Wooten said, "You learn more from losing than winning. You learn to keep going." Adds Yoda, "In a dark place we find ourselves, and a little more knowledge lights our way."

The art of great leadership requires a continuous evaluation of one's own leadership skills, mindset, philosophy, actions, and development.

Confidence is another key component of being a great leader, provided it is held in check and not seen as self-promoting, ego-centric boosterism. All three of our leadership brain trust characters exude confidence, though at times Captain Sparrow edges toward being a bit over-board:

> *"When you marooned me on that godforsaken spit of island you forgot one thing...I'm Captain Jack Sparrow."* (In reply to a question on how he got off a deserted island.)
>
> *"I'm Captain Jack Sparrow. The original. The only."*

Confidence in your skills and abilities will reduce stress and pressure, leading to better analysis, evaluation, and decision making. Even Yoda knows this, sharing that "You will know (the good from the bad) when you are clam, at peace. Passive. A Jedi uses the Force for knowledge and defense, never for attack." Even if the Force is not with you, self-confidence and trust in your capabilities will aid you as a leader.

Understanding the art of great leadership will help prevent you from tripping and falling as your pursue your leadership journey.

**Final Words**
It has been a pleasure sharing an overview of my thinking and beliefs on how to become, and remain, a great leader.

For more thoughts, tools, tips, and ideas on great leadership, please visit my blog at:

> CalienteLeadership.com/TheArtofGreatLeadershipBlog

For now, however, let's allow our leadership brain trust trio to share their final words of wisdom:

> **Special Agent Gibbs**
> *Some times you're wrong.* (Rule 51)

*I was doing something wrong. And when something's wrong, you change it.*

*Not doing the right thing, because you have nothing to lose or gain, that just makes you a bad person.*

*You cannot let personal situations color your judgment.*

*I've seen bad turn to good plenty of times. You just can't lose faith.*

*A leader looks after his men. Fights for them.*

*A slap to the face is an insult — to the back of the head is a wake-up call.*

*You do something good now, you're not always around to see the difference it makes later.*

*You bring pride to the job, people notice. And even if they don't, you notice.*

*Trust. Loyalty. They're important.*

*Don't let a bad situation define who you are.*

*Never second guess yourself in a relationship and life.*

**Yoda**
*Fear is the path to the dark side. Fear leads to anger. Anger leads to hate. Hate leads to suffering.*

*To be Jedi is to face the truth, and choose. Give off light, or darkness, Padawan. Be a candle, or the night.*

*Do or do not. There is no try.*

*May the Force be with you.*


**Captain Jack Sparrow**
*My spirit will live on.*

*I regret nothing, ever.*

# APPENDIX

# Steven Howard's Personal Leadership Philosophy

Leadership is an art.

It is the art of achieving progress through the involvement and actions of others.

Successful leaders apply the skills of adaptability, motivation, coaching, focus, collaboration, decision-making, communications, and personal development to both themselves and the people they lead.

Strong leaders leverage the emotions of passion, enthusiasm, self-satisfaction, trust, and loyalty to drive creativity, thinking, innovation, energy, and buy-in to strategies, tactics, and activities in pursuit of clearly stated goals and objectives.

# Steven Howard's
# Rules of Great Leadership

1. Leadership is about both people and results. If you have to neglect one, neglect the results for these will come in time when you have developed your people.

2. Great leaders are great listeners. They know they learn more from listening than from speaking.

3. Great leaders happen at all levels of an organization, not just in the executive suites or ownership ranks.

4. People development is the single most important long-term priority and responsibility of all leaders, at all levels of an organization. Great leaders ensure that this happens.

5. Great leaders are made, through circumstances, experiences, reflection, and skill enhancement.

6. Great leadership is honed by reflection, mindfulness, compassion, and action. It is enhanced via continuous learning and improvement.

7. When great leadership is exhibited at all levels of an organization, competitive advantage ensues.

8. Great leaders create more leaders, not just followers.

9. Great leaders know they cannot lead everyone. Some people may not want to be led by them. When this happens agree to go your separate ways respectfully.

10. Great leadership is achieving results through others while enhancing the skills and talents of team members.

11. A focus on people development is one of the most important factors that differentiates great leaders from good leaders.

12. Great leaders practice Leadership Accountability, holding themselves and other leaders accountable for their leadership behaviors, actions and for making ethical decisions.

13. Great leaders devote significant energy and time clarifying and understanding the perspectives, ideas, concerns, and questions of others.

14. Great leaders do not see clarification questions from team members and peers as push-back.

15. Great leaders assert their right to express their viewpoints, concerns and questions to senior leaders

and team members in a professional and respectful manner.

16. The leadership behaviors of great leaders is almost always fully congruent with their self understood and deeply believed leadership philosophy and leadership mindset. And incongruences are usually the exceptions that prove the rule.

17. Everyone needs a code they can lead by. That is why great leaders have their own written leadership philosophy that strongly influences how they interpret reality and guides them on how to react to people, events and situations.

# Gibbs Rules

Rule 1: Never let suspects stay together.

Rule 1: Never screw over your partner. [Note: there are two Rule #1s]

Rule 2: Always wear gloves at a crime scene.

Rule 3: Don't believe what you're told. Double check.

Rule 3: Never be unreachable. [Note: there are two Rule #3s]

Rule 4: The best way to keep a secret? Keep it to yourself. Second best? Tell one other person — if you must. There is no third best.

Rule 5: You don't waste good.

Rule 6: Never say you're sorry. It's a sign of weakness.

Rule 7: Always be specific when you lie.

Rule 8: Never take anything for granted. [Also quoted in one episode as "Never assume."]

Rule 9: Never go anywhere without a knife.

Rule 10: Never get personally involved in a case.

Rule 11: When the job is done, walk away.

Rule 12: Never date a co-worker.

Rule 13: Never, ever involve lawyers.

Rule 14: Bend the line, don't break it.

Rule 15: Always work as a team.

Rule 16: If someone thinks they have the upper hand, break it.

Rule 18: It's better to seek forgiveness than ask permission.

Rule 20: Always look under.

Rule 22: Never ever bother Gibbs in interrogation.

Rule 23: Never mess with a Marine's coffee... if you want to live.

Rule 27: There are two ways to follow someone. First way, they never notice you. Second way, they *only* notice you.

Rule 28: When you need help, ask.

Rule 35: Always watch the watchers.

Rule 36: If you feel like you are being played, you probably are.

Rule 38: Your case, your lead.

Rule 39: There is no such thing as coincidence.

Rule 40: If it seems like someone is out to get you, they are.

Rule 42: Never accept an apology from someone who just sucker punched you.

Rule 44: First things first, hide the women and children.

Rule 45: Clean up the mess that you make. [Note: This rule is also stated in one episode as "Never leave behind loose ends."]

Rule 51: Sometimes you're wrong.

Rule 62: Always give space to people getting off an elevator.

Rule 69: Never trust a woman who doesn't trust her man.


*Other statements that could be considered rules, but are not written down as such:*

In my country, on my team, working my cases, my people don't bypass the chain of command.

You do what you have to do for family.

Don't work the system when you can work the people.

Don't stop checking and rechecking evidence until you are satisfied.

If you want to find something, you follow it.

Never second guess yourself in a relationship and life.

A slap to the face is an insult — to the back of the head is a wake-up call.

## Yoda Quotes

1) Train yourself to let go of everything you fear to lose.

2) Fear is the path to the dark side. Fear leads to anger. Anger leads to hate. Hate leads to suffering.

3) Death is a natural part of life. Rejoice for those around you who transform into the Force. Mourn them do not. Miss them do not. Attachment leads to jealously. The shadow of greed, that is.

4) Always pass on what you have learned.

5) You will know (the good from the bad) when you are calm, at peace. Passive. A Jedi uses the Force for knowledge and defense, never for attack.

6) [Luke:] I can't believe it. [Yoda:] That is why you fail.

7) Yes, a Jedi's strength flows from the Force. But beware of the dark side. Anger, fear, aggression; the dark side of the Force are they. Easily they flow, quick to join you in a fight.

8) Powerful you have become, the dark side I sense in you.

9) If you end your training now — if you choose the quick and easy path as Vader did — you will become an agent of evil.

10) Patience you must have my young Padawan.

11) Ready are you? What know you of ready? For eight hundred years have I trained Jedi. My own counsel will I keep on who is to be trained. A Jedi must have the deepest commitment, the most serious mind.

12) Feel the Force!

13) Once you start down the dark path, forever will it dominate your destiny, consume you it will.

14) You must unlearn what you have learned.

15) In a dark place we find ourselves, and a little more knowledge lights our way.

16) When you look at the dark side, careful you must be. For the dark side looks back.

17) Many of the truths that we cling to depend on our point of view.

18) Through the Force, things you will see. Other places. The future...the past. Old friends long gone.

19) Truly wonderful the mind of a child is.

20) The fear of loss is a path to the Dark Side.

21) A Jedi must have the deepest commitment, the most serious mind.

22) Do or do not. There is no try.

23) You will find only what you bring in.

24) May the Force be with you.

25) Size matters not. Look at me. Judge me by my size, do you? Hmm? Hmm. And well you should not.

26) Ohhh. Great warrior. Wars not make one great.

27) Always two there are, no more, no less. A master and an apprentice.

28) Difficult to see. Always in motion is the future.

29) I have many children, as you seek you may find that this the last one till he must die before he must reach the becoming of mankind. Many men have failed but I have surpassed their expectation of being a Jedi master.

30) Looking? Found someone you have, eh?

31) If into the security recordings you go, only pain will you find.

32) You think Yoda stops teaching, just because his student does not want to hear? A teacher Yoda is. Yoda teaches like drunkards drink, like killers kill.

33) [Luke:] What's in there? [Yoda:] Only what you take with you.

34) Happens to every guy sometimes this does.

35) Foreplay, cuddling – a Jedi craves not these things.

36) The dark side clouds everything. Impossible to see the future is.

37) Not if anything to say about it I have.

38) Named must your fear be before banish it you can.

39) Soon will I rest, yes, forever sleep. Earned it I have. Twilight is upon me, soon night must fall.

40) Lost a planet Master Obi-Wan has. How embarrassing.

41) At an end your rule is, and not short enough it was!

42) Do not assume anything Obi-Wan. Clear your mind must be if you are to discover the real villains behind this plot.

43) Mudhole? Slimy? My home this is!

44) When nine hundred years old you reach, look as good, you will not, hmmmm?

45) Reckless he is. Matters are worse.

46) Much to learn you still have...my old Padawan. This is just the beginning!

47) Ow, ow, OW! On my ear you are!

48) Early must I rise. Leave now you must!

49) If no mistake have you made, yet losing you are...a different game you should play.

50) I was not strong enough to defeat him. Like his master before him, be destroyed, he must.

51) Good relations with the Wookiees, I have.

52) Ahhh! Yoda's little friend you seek!

53) Mine, or I will help you not!

54) The boy you trained, gone he is. Consumed by Darth Vader.

55) Who's your Jedi master? WHO'S your Jedi Master?

56) Stopped they must be; on this all depends. Only a fully-trained Jedi Knight, with the Force as his ally, will conquer Vader and his Emperor.

57) Use your feelings, Obi-Wan, and find him you will.

58) Urm. Put a shield on my saber I must.

59) Strong is Vader. Mind what you have learned. Save you it can.

60) Faith in your new apprentice, misplaced may be. As is your faith in the dark side of the Force.

61) Decide you must, how to serve them best. If you leave now, help them you could; but you would destroy all for which they have fought, and suffered.

62) To answer power with power, the Jedi way this is not. In this war, a danger there is, of losing who we are.

63) Secret, shall I tell you? Grand Master of Jedi Order am I. Won this job in a raffle I did, think you? "How did you know, how did you know, Master Yoda?" Master Yoda knows these things. His job it is.

64) For my ally is the Force. And a powerful ally it is. Life creates it, makes it grow. Its energy surrounds us and binds us. Luminous beings are we...not this crude

matter. You must feel the Force around you. Here, between you...me...the tree...the rock...everywhere! Yes, even between this land and that ship!

65) To be Jedi is to face the truth, and choose. Give off light, or darkness, Padawan. Be a candle, or the night.

66) On many long journeys have I gone. And waited, too, for others to return from journeys of their own. Some return; some are broken; some come back so different only their names remain.

67) I cannot teach him. The boy has no patience.

68) Control, control, you must learn control!

69) Blind we are, if creation of this clone army we could not see.

70) Already know you that which you need.

71) Hmm. In the end, cowards are those who follow the dark side.

# Capt'n Jack Sparrow Quotes

1) My spirit will live on.

2) Not all treasure is silver and gold mate.

3) You've stolen me and I'm here to take myself back.

4) If you choose to lock your heart away, you'll lose it for certain.

5) Why fight when you can negotiate?

6) Wherever we want to go, we go. That's what a ship is, you know. It's not just a keel and hull and a deck and sails. That's what a ship needs. But what a ship is....what the Black Pearl really is.....is freedom.

7) The seas may be rough, but I am the Captain! No matter how difficult, I will always prevail.

8) The problem is not the problem. The problem is your attitude about the problem. Do you understand?

9) The only rules that really matter are these: what a man can do and what a man can't do.

10) I regret nothing, ever.

11) Better to not know which moment may be your last, alive to be mystery of it all.

12) Close your eyes and pretend it's all a bad dream. That's how I get by.

13) Did everyone see that? Because I will not be doing it again.

14) The world's still the same. There's just less in it.

15) And me, for example, I can let you drown, but I can't bring this ship into Tortuga all by me onesies, savvy? So, can you sail under the command of a pirate?

16) Did no one come to save me just because they missed me?

17) Batten down the hatches, mates, it's gonna get ugly! Relatively speaking.

18) Well done, mates. I knew you had it in you. Now, come back in eight minutes and we'll do it all over again, eh?

19) I think this situation is what one might call a "pickle." MMMM, pickles be tasty sometimes.

20) I say, to hell with the Cutler Becketts of this world, and to hell with their so-called "legal" ways of doing business. Once a pirate, always a pirate. I know that

now, and I swear from now on, it's the pirate life for me.

21) This is either madness or brilliance. It's remarkable how often those two coincide.

22) Take what you can. Give nothin' back.

23) When you marooned me on that godforsaken spit of land you forgot one thing mate....I'm Captain Jack Sparrow. [In reply to the question: "How the blazes did you get off that island?"]

24) If we don't have the key, we can't open whatever it is we don't have that it unlocks. So what purpose would be served in finding whatever need be unlocked, which we don't have, without first having found the key what unlocks it?

25) Remember, he who fights and runs away, lives to run away again.

26) Thank goodness for that, because if I wasn't, this would probably never work. [In reply to a comment that Sparrow "is mad."]

27) I'm Captain Jack Sparrow. The original. The only.

28) It's not the destination so much as the journey, they say.

29) I wonder.....does it work because it works, or because you believe that it works?

30) If you were waiting for the opportune moment, that was it.

31) Wherever we want to go, we'll go.

32) This is the day you will always remember as the day you almost caught Captain Jack Sparrow.

now, and I swear from now on, it's the pirate life for me.

21) This is either madness or brilliance. It's remarkable how often those two coincide.

22) Take what you can. Give nothin' back.

23) When you marooned me on that godforsaken spit of land you forgot one thing mate....I'm Captain Jack Sparrow. [In reply to the question: "How the blazes did you get off that island?"]

24) If we don't have the key, we can't open whatever it is we don't have that it unlocks. So what purpose would be served in finding whatever need be unlocked, which we don't have, without first having found the key what unlocks it?

25) Remember, he who fights and runs away, lives to run away again.

26) Thank goodness for that, because if I wasn't, this would probably never work. [In reply to a comment that Sparrow "is mad."]

27) I'm Captain Jack Sparrow. The original. The only.

28) It's not the destination so much as the journey, they say.

29) I wonder.....does it work because it works, or because you believe that it works?

30) If you were waiting for the opportune moment, that was it.

31) Wherever we want to go, we'll go.

32) This is the day you will always remember as the day you almost caught Captain Jack Sparrow.

# About the Author

**Steven B. Howard**
**Global Leadership Development Facilitation | Leadership Coach | Keynote Speaker**

Steven Howard specializes in creating and deliverying Leadership Development curriculum for frontline leaders, mid-level leaders, senior leaders and high-potential leaders.

An author with 36 years of international senior sales, marketing, and leadership experience, his corporate career covered a wide variety of fields and experiences, including Regional Marketing Director for Texas Instruments Asia-Pacific, South Asia & ASEAN Regional Director for TIME Magazine, Global Account Director at BBDO Advertising handling an international airline account, and VP Marketing for Citibank's Consumer Banking Group.

Since 1988 he has delivered leadership development training programs in the U.S., Asia, Australia, Africa, and Europe to numerous organizations, including Citicorp, Covidien, DBS Bank, Deutsche Bank, Dupont Lycra, Esso Productions, ExxonMobil, Hewlett Packard, Micron Technology, Motorola Solutions, SapientNitro, Standard Chartered Bank, and many others.

He has been a member of the training faculty at MasterCard University Asia/Pacific, the Citibank Asia-Pacific Banking Institute, and Forum Corporation. He brings a truly international, cross-cultural perspective to his leadership development programs, having lived in the USA for 26 years, in Singapore for 21 years and in Australia for 12 years.

In addition to his leadership facilitation work Steven has served on several Boards in both the private and non-profit sectors. He has also chaired a strategic advisory group for a local government entity and a national sporting organization that is a member of the Australian Olympic Committee.

Steven is the author of 11 marketing and management books and is the editor of three professional and personal development books in the Project You series.

His other books are:

>**Corporate Image Management:** *A Marketing Discipline*
>
>**Powerful Marketing Minutes:** *50 Ways to Develop Market Leadership*
>
>**MORE Powerful Marketing Minutes:** *50 New Ways to Develop Market Leadership*
>
>**Asian Words of Wisdom**
>
>**Asian Words of Knowledge**

*Essential Asian Words of Wisdom*

*Pillars of Growth: Strategies for Leading Sustainable Growth* (co-author with three others)

*Motivation Plus Marketing Equals Money* (co-author with four others)

*Marketing Words of Wisdom*

*The Best of the Monday Morning Marketing Memo*

*Powerful Marketing Memos*

## Contact Details

Email: steven@CalienteLeadership.com

Twitter: @stevenbhoward | @GreatLeadershp

LinkedIn: www.linkedin.com/in/stevenbhoward

Facebook: www.facebook.com/CalienteLeadership

Website: www.CalienteLeadership.com

Blog: CalienteLeadership.com/TheArtofGreatLeadershipBlog